32

D0824616

I have feelings
Tengo sentimientos

Bobbie Kalman

Crabtree Publishing Company

www.crabtreebooks.com

Created by Bobbie Kalman

Author and Editor-in-Chief
Bobbie Kalman

Educational consultants
Joan King
Reagan Miller
Elaine Hurst

Editors
Joan King
Reagan Miller
Kathy Middleton

Proofreader
Crystal Sikkens

Design
Bobbie Kalman
Katherine Berti

Photo research
Bobbie Kalman

Production coordinator
Katherine Berti

Prepress technician
Katherine Berti

Photographs by Shutterstock

Library and Archives Canada Cataloguing in Publication

Kalman, Bobbie, 1947-
 I have feelings = Tengo sentimientos / Bobbie Kalman.

(My world = Mi mundo)
Issued also in an electronic format.
Text in English and Spanish.
ISBN 978-0-7787-8272-8 (bound).--ISBN 978-0-7787-8265-0 (pbk.)

 1. Emotions--Juvenile literature. I. Title. II. Title: Tengo sentimientos.
III. Series: My world (St. Catharines, Ont.) IV. Series: Mi mundo (St.
Catharines, Ont.)

BF561.K34 2011   j152.4   C2010-904284-0

Library of Congress Cataloging-in-Publication Data

Kalman, Bobbie.
 [I have feelings Spanish & English]
 I have feelings = Tengo sentimientos / Bobbie Kalman.
  p. cm. -- (My world = Mi mundo)
 ISBN 978-0-7787-8265-0 (pbk. : alk. paper) -- ISBN 978-0-7787-8272-8 (reinforced
library binding : alk. paper) -- ISBN 978-1-4271-9591-3 (electronic (pdf))
 1. Emotions--Juvenile literature. I. Title. II. Title: Tengo sentimientos. III. Series.

BF511.K35 2011
152.4--dc22

                          2010024903

Crabtree Publishing Company

www.crabtreebooks.com   1-800-387-7650

Printed in Hong Kong/042011/BK20110304

Copyright © **2011 CRABTREE PUBLISHING COMPANY**. All rights reserved. No part of this publication may be reproduced, stored in a retrieval system or be transmitted in any form or by any means, electronic, mechanical, photocopying, recording, or otherwise, without the prior written permission of Crabtree Publishing Company. In Canada: We acknowledge the financial support of the Government of Canada through the Canada Book Fund for our publishing activities.

Published in Canada
Crabtree Publishing
616 Welland Ave.
St. Catharines, Ontario
L2M 5V6

Published in the United States
Crabtree Publishing
PMB 59051
350 Fifth Avenue, 59th Floor
New York, New York 10118

Published in the United Kingdom
Crabtree Publishing
Maritime House
Basin Road North, Hove
BN41 1WR

Published in Australia
Crabtree Publishing
386 Mt. Alexander Rd.
Ascot Vale (Melbourne)
VIC 3032

Words to know
Palabras que debo saber

angry   mad   brave   happy
enojado furioso valiente feliz

proud   sad   scared   silly
orgulloso triste asustado gracioso

I am feeling happy.

Me siento feliz.

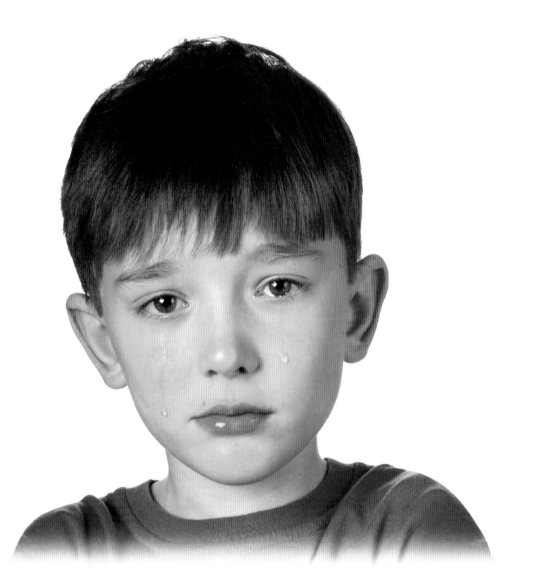

I am feeling sad.

Me siento triste.

I am feeling angry.

Me siento enojado.

I am feeling mad.

Me siento furioso.

I am feeling scared.

Me siento asustado.

I am feeling brave.

Soy valiente.

I am feeling silly.

Soy gracioso.

I am feeling proud.

Me siento orgulloso.

I like these feelings.
happy   brave   proud   silly
Me gustan estos sentimientos.
feliz   valiente orgulloso gracioso

I do not like these feelings.

sad   mad   angry   scared

No me gustan estos sentimientos.

triste   furioso   enojado   asustado

Activity
Do you have these feelings?

surprised
sorprendido

Actividad
¿Cómo te sientes?

smart
listo

ashamed
avergonzado

excited
emocionado

confused
confundido

joyful
alegre

beautiful
hermoso

great
genial

wonderful
maravilloso

amazing
asombrado

glad
contento

confident
seguro

Notes for adults

Talking about feelings
This book introduces children to the feelings they might like or dislike. Ask them to describe how it feels to be happy, sad, mad, proud, silly, confident, confused, ashamed, or excited. Have them name some events that trigger certain feelings or emotions. Talking about feelings is a good way to understand that feelings, whether they make us feel good or bad, are normal.

Act it out!
Write the vocabulary words about feelings introduced in the book on index cards. Write one feeling on each card. Lay the cards face down. Have children take turns picking a card and then acting out the emotion using facial expressions, body language, and actions. The other children can guess which emotion the student is showing. The pictures in this book will make them aware of some facial expressions and body language that correspond with certain feelings.

Color your feelings
Show some sheets of colored paper to your students. Ask them to describe their feelings when they see each of the colors. Does pink make them feel happy and blue make them feel sad? Read out the feelings vocabulary in this book and ask them which color best describes each feeling.

Notas para los adultos

Hablar sobre los sentimientos
Este libro presenta a los niños sentimientos que tal vez les gusten o no. Pídales que describan qué se siente al estar feliz, triste, furioso, orgulloso, gracioso, seguro, confundido, avergonzado o emocionado. Pídales que nombren algunos sucesos que provocan ciertos sentimientos o ciertas emociones. Hablar sobre los sentimientos es una buena manera de comprender que los sentimientos, ya sea que nos hagan sentir bien o mal, son algo normal.

¡Represéntalo!
Escriba en tarjetas las palabras de vocabulario sobre sentimientos que se presentaron en este libro. Escriba un sentimiento en cada tarjeta. Coloque las tarjetas boca abajo. Pida a los niños que se turnen para escoger una tarjeta y luego representen la emoción con expresiones faciales, lenguaje corporal y acciones. Los otros niños pueden adivinar qué emoción muestra el estudiante. Las fotos de este libro les harán darse cuenta de las expresiones faciales y el lenguaje corporal que corresponden a ciertos sentimientos.

Colorea tus sentimientos
Muestre a sus estudiantes algunas hojas de papel de colores. Pídales que describan lo que sienten al ver cada uno de los colores. ¿El color rosado los hace sentirse felices y el azul los hace sentirse tristes? Lea en voz alta el vocabulario de los sentimientos que aparecen en este libro y pregúnteles qué color describe mejor cada sentimiento.

Pine River Library
395 Bayfield Center Dr.
P.O. Box 227
Bayfield, CO 81122
(970) 884-2222
www.prlibrary.org